Table of Contents

As humans we live in our **Minds**

Understanding The Human Mind: The Big Picture

The mind is its own place
and in itself
can make a hell of heaven
or a heaven of hell
John Milton

Everyone thinks. It is our nature to do so. But much of our thinking left to itself is biased, distorted, ill-founded, or prejudiced. Much of our thinking leads to problems in our lives. Much of our thinking leads to cruelty and injustice. Of course, the mind doesn't just think, it also feels and wants. What is the connection? Our thinking shapes and determines how we feel and what we want. When we think well, we are motivated to do things that make sense and motivated to act in ways that help rather than harm ourselves and others.

At the same time, powerful emotions or desires influence our thinking, help or hinder how well we think in a situation. At any given moment, our minds (that complex of inner thoughts, feelings and desires) can be under the sway of our native egocentrism or our potential reasonability. When we are ruled by our egocentric tendencies, we see the world from a narrow self-serving perspective. We are not truly concerned with how our behavior affects others. We are fundamentally concerned with getting what we want and/or with validating our beliefs and views.

The key to understanding human thought then, is, to understand its essential duality: its capacity for egocentrism (being trapped in self-delusion, myth, and illusion) and its capacity for reasonability (freeing itself from self-delusion, myth, and illusion).

Though thinking, feeling and wanting are, in principle, equally important, it is only through thinking that we take command of our minds. It is through thinking that we figure out what is going wrong with our thinking. It is through thinking that we figure out how to deal with destructive emotions. It is through thinking that we change unproductive desires to productive ones. It is fair-minded reasonability that frees us from intellectual slavery.

If we understand our mind and its functions, if we face the barriers to our development that egocentrism represents, if we work upon our mind in a daily regimen, we can take the steps that lead to our empowerment as thinkers.

The Mind's Three Distinctive Functions

The mind has three basic functions: thinking, feeling, and wanting.

- <u>Thinking</u> is the part of the mind that figures things out. It makes sense of life's events. It creates the ideas through which we define situations, relationships and problems. It continually tells us: This is what is going on. This is what is happening. Notice this and that.

- <u>Feelings</u>* are created by thinking — evaluating whether the events of our lives are positive or negative. Feelings continually tell us: "This is how I should feel about what is happening in my life. I'm doing really well." Or, alternatively, "Things aren't going well for me."

- Our <u>desires</u> allocate energy to action, in keeping with what we define as desirable and possible. It continually tells us: "This is worth getting. Go for it!" Or, conversely, "This is not worth getting. Don't bother."

---

* When we speak of feelings, we are not referring to emotions caused by dysfunctional biological processes such as problems in brain chemistry. When emotions are caused by imbalances in brain chemistry which people cannot control themselves, clinical help may be needed. When we speak of feelings, we are also not referring to bodily sensations, though feelings often accompany bodily sensations. For instance being "cold" might cause you to feel irritable. Recognizing the feeling of irritability might lead you to do something about being cold, like putting on a jacket. Finally, though the terms "feelings" and "emotions" might be used in some cases to refer to different phenomena, we use these terms interchangeably in this guide.

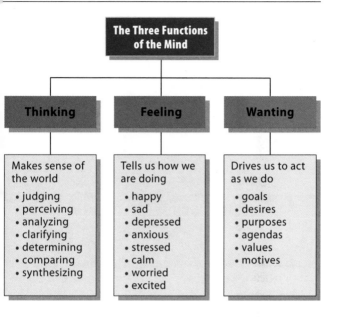

Essential Idea: Our mind is continually communicating three kinds of things to us:

1) what is going on in life,

2) feelings (positive or negative) about those events, and

3) things to pursue, where to put our energy (in light of 1 and 2).

The Dynamic Relationship Between Thinking, Feeling, Wanting

There is an intimate, dynamic interrelation between thinking, feeling, and wanting. Each is continually influencing the other two.

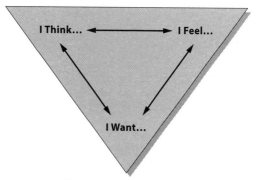

For example, when we *think* we are being threatened, we *feel* fear, and we inevitably *want* to flee from or attack whatever we think is threatening us. When we *feel* depressed, we *think* that there is nothing we can do to improve our situation, and we therefore *lack the motivation* to do anything about our situation. When we *want* to improve our eating habits it may be because we *think* that our diet is causing us harm and we *feel* dissatisfied with our diet.

Though we can consider the functions of the mind separately (to better understand them), they can never be absolutely separated. Imagine them as a triangle with three necessary sides: thoughts, feelings and desires. Eliminate one side of the triangle and it collapses. Each side depends on the other two. In other words, without thinking there can be no feelings or desires; without feelings, no thoughts or desires; without desires, no thoughts or feelings. For example, it is unintelligible to imagine *thinking* that something is threatening you and might harm you, *wanting* to escape from it, yet *feeling* nothing in relationship to what you think and want. Because you *think* you might be harmed and you *want* to flee, you necessarily *feel* fear.

Behavior: A Product of the Mind's Functions

Thoughts, feelings and desires continually interact, and produce behavior as a result of that interaction. To understand this, consider the example on the previous page about eating habits. Suppose you feel dissatisfied with your diet. You want to improve your diet because you think that by doing so you will improve your health.

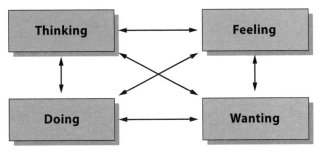

You therefore *behave* in the following ways:

1. read about different diets (behavior),
2. come to conclusions about the best diet for you, then ***change your diet*** accordingly.

After a few weeks you notice that you feel better physically and are losing weight. You now feel satisfied. You *think* that your diet is improving your health. You therefore *want* to continue with the new diet.

But then after a few more weeks you *think:* "I don't *want* to eat any more salads and tasteless foods. I can't keep this up for the rest of my life! There must be a diet available that is not boring." You therefore *act* on that thinking. Again you consider different diet possibilities, finally deciding upon a new diet. The process begins again, with thoughts, feelings, desires, continually shaping behavior.

    www.criticalthinking.org

Thinking as the Key to Feelings and Desires

Though thoughts, feelings and desires play equally important roles in the mind, continually influencing and being influenced by one another, thinking is the key to command of feelings and desires. To change a feeling is to change the thinking that leads to the feeling. To change a desire is to change the thinking that underlies the desire.

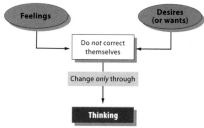

If I feel angry because my child is behaving disrespectfully toward me, I can't simply replace anger with satisfaction, for example. To change the anger to a more positive emotion, I must change the thinking I am doing in the situation. Perhaps I need to think about how to teach my child to behave respectfully towards me, and then behave in accordance with that new thinking. Perhaps I need to think about the influences in my child's life that might be causing the rude behavior and then try to eliminate those influences. In other words, I get control of my emotional state through my thinking.

Similarly we can't change a desire without changing the thinking that causes the desire. Suppose, for example, two people, Jan and John, have been in a romantic relationship but John has broken off the relationship. Yet Jan still wants to be in the relationship. Suppose that her desire comes from thinking (that may be unconscious) that she needs to be in the relationship to be emotionally stable, that she won't be able to function without John. Clearly this thinking is the problem. Jan must therefore change her thinking so she no longer wants a relationship with John. In other words, until she thinks that she does not need John to be OK, that she can function satisfactorily without him, that she doesn't need to be in a relationship with a person who doesn't want to be with her, she will want to be in the relationship with John. In short, unless her thinking changes, her desire won't change. She must defeat the thinking that is defeating her.

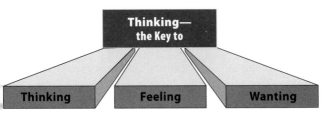

Thinking—
the Key to

| Thinking | Feeling | Wanting |

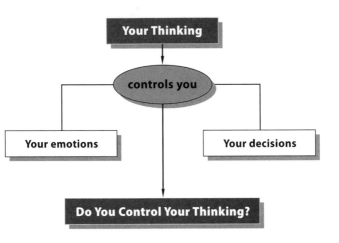

Your Thinking

controls you

Your emotions

Your decisions

Do You Control Your Thinking?

Rational Capacities or Egocentric Tendencies Control the Mind

The three functions of the mind — thoughts, feelings and desires — can be guided or directed either by one's native egocentrism or by one's potential rational capacities. Egocentric tendencies function automatically and unconsciously. Rational tendencies arise only from active self-development and are largely conscious.

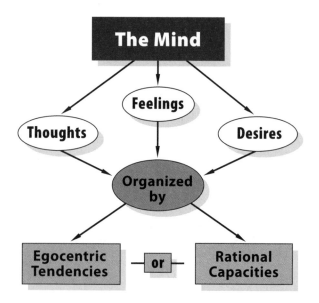

The Problem of Egocentric Thinking

Egocentric thinking comes from the unfortunate fact that humans do not naturally consider the rights and needs of others, nor do we naturally appreciate the point of view of others or the limitations in our own point of view. We become explicitly aware of our egocentric thinking only if trained to do so. We do not naturally recognize our egocentric assumptions, the egocentric way we use information, the egocentric way we interpret data, the source of our egocentric concepts and ideas, the implications of our egocentric thought. We do not naturally recognize our self-serving perspective.

As humans we live with the unrealistic but confident sense that we have fundamentally figured out *the way things actually are,* and that we have done this objectively. We naturally *believe* in our intuitive *perceptions*—however inaccurate. Instead of using intellectual standards in thinking, we often use self-centered psychological standards to determine what to believe and what to reject. Here are the most commonly used psychological standards in human thinking:

"IT'S TRUE BECAUSE *I* BELIEVE IT." *Innate egocentrism:* I assume that what I believe is true even though I have never questioned the basis for many of my beliefs.

"IT'S TRUE BECAUSE *WE* BELIEVE IT." *Innate sociocentrism:* I assume that the dominant beliefs within the groups to which I belong are true even though I have never questioned the basis for many of these beliefs.

"IT'S TRUE BECAUSE I *WANT* TO BELIEVE IT." *Innate wish fulfillment:* I believe in, for example, accounts of behavior that put me (or the groups to which I belong) in a positive rather than a negative light even though I have not seriously considered the evidence for the more negative account. I believe what "feels good," what supports my other beliefs, what does not require me to change my thinking in any significant way, what does not require me to admit I have been wrong.

"IT'S TRUE BECAUSE I *HAVE ALWAYS* BELIEVED IT." *Innate self-validation:* I have a strong desire to maintain beliefs that I have long held, even though I have not seriously considered the extent to which those beliefs are justified, given the evidence.

"IT'S TRUE BECAUSE IT IS *IN MY SELFISH INTEREST* TO BELIEVE IT." *Innate selfishness:* I hold fast to beliefs that justify my getting more power, money, or personal advantage even though these beliefs are not grounded in sound reasoning or evidence.

Since humans are naturally prone to assess thinking in keeping with the above criteria, it is not surprising that we, as a species, have not developed a significant interest in establishing and teaching legitimate intellectual standards. It is not surprising that our thinking is often flawed.

Distinguish Egocentric From Rational Motives

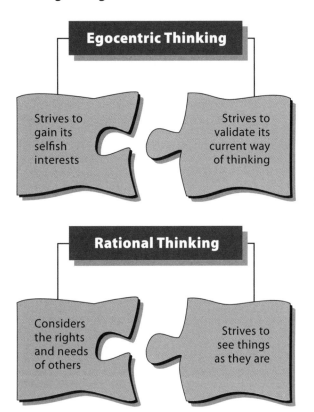

Egocentric Thinking

Strives to gain its selfish interests

Strives to validate its current way of thinking

Rational Thinking

Considers the rights and needs of others

Strives to see things as they are

Egocentricity

Exists in two forms: skilled and unskilled. Both pursue selfish ends.

Highly skilled egocentric persons use their intelligence to effectively rationalize gaining their selfish ends at the expense of others. They skillfully distort information to serve their interest. They are often articulate in arguing for their ends (which they typically cover with altruistic language). They hide their prejudices well. Naïve others often fail to see their selfish core (masked, as it is, in an ethical or seemingly considerate façade). They often succeed in moving up the social ladder and gain prestigious jobs and honored positions. Skilled egocentric persons may favor either domination or submission, but often combine both in effective ways. For example, they may successfully dominate persons "below" them while they are subtly servile to those "above" them. They know how to tell people what they want to hear. They are consummate manipulators and often hold positions of power.

Unskilled egocentric persons are unsuccessful in pursuing their selfish ends because many see through them and do not trust them. Their prejudices and narrowness are more obvious and less schooled. They often have blatantly dysfunctional relationships with others. They are often trapped in negative emotions that they do not understand. Unskilled egocentric persons may prefer either domination or submission as a means of getting what they want, but whichever they use, they are usually unsuccessful at either. Sometimes they are overtly cruel or play the victim in openly self-pitying ways.

Rationality

Rationality is sometimes wrongly thought of as covering both those who intelligently and successfully pursue selfish ends and those who intelligently and successfully pursue unselfish ends. We believe that those who intelligently pursue selfish ends are precisely those described above as skilled egocentric persons. In other words, we do not think that those who sophistically manipulate people to act against their interests and consequently lack integrity, are properly called "reasonable" persons. Consummate manipulators, however skilled and successful, are not reasonable persons (since they would be the first to object to being treated as they routinely treat others).

Rationality is properly thought of as a way of thinking and acting in which intelligence and sound reasoning are used to serve justice, in which the actor adheres to the same standards by which he judges his enemy, in which he does not need to rationalize or project a false façade to impress others. Successful powerful people are often intelligent, unreason-able, and unscrupulous—all in one. They often cannot openly admit the games they play to obtain social and economic success. They often suppress evidence that puts them in a bad light. To us, reasonable people, on the other hand, respect the rights and needs of others, are flexible, open-minded, and just. They have intellectual integrity as well as intellectual humility and perseverance. They have confidence in reason and follow its lead. They are able to enter empathically into the point of view of others. They do not misuse language. They say what they mean and mean what they say.

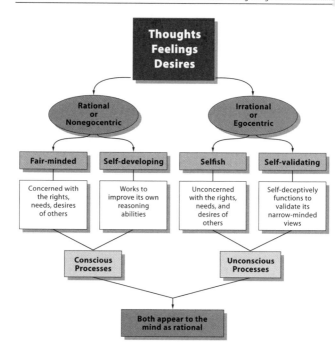

Essential Idea: Human rationality is fair-minded and self-developing while irrationality (or egocentrism) is selfish and self-validating. All irrationality presupposes some degree of unconsciousness in order to function self-deceptively. Most rational thought functions consciously. Because irrationality appears to the mind as reasonable, we must develop strategies for disclosing irrational thought.

Feelings That Accompany Egocentrism

These are some of the many feelings that might accompany egocentric thinking. They often occur when egocentric thinking is "unsuccessful."

Essential Idea: When egocentric thinking is successful in getting what it wants, positive feelings accompany it. But when egocentric thinking is not able to achieve its purposes, negative feelings result.

The Logic of Egocentrism

Egocentrism has a self-contained logic. To itself, it appears logical. By focusing on its logic we can figure out how it functions. We can figure out its purpose, assumptions, point of view, etc.[1]

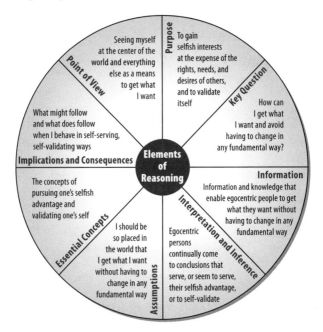

---

[1] An overview of the elements of reasoning, which provide a structure for understanding this logic and the others in this miniguide, can be found in the *Miniature Guide to Critical Thinking Concepts and Tools.* See page 32.

The Logic of Rationality

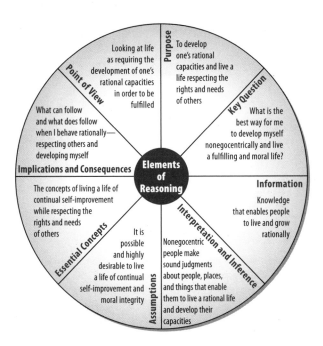

Elements of Reasoning

Purpose
To develop one's rational capacities and live a life respecting the rights and needs of others

Key Question
What is the best way for me to develop myself nonegocentrically and live a fulfilling and moral life?

Information
Knowledge that enables people to live and grow rationally

Interpretation and Inference
Nonegocentric people make sound judgments about people, places, and things that enable them to live a rational life and develop their capacities

Assumptions
It is possible and highly desirable to live a life of continual self-improvement and moral integrity

Essential Concepts
The concepts of living a life of continual self-improvement while respecting the rights and needs of others

Implications and Consequences
What can follow and what does follow when I behave rationally—respecting others and developing myself

Point of View
Looking at life as requiring the development of one's rational capacities in order to be fulfilled

Distinguishing Egocentric Domination From Egocentric Submission

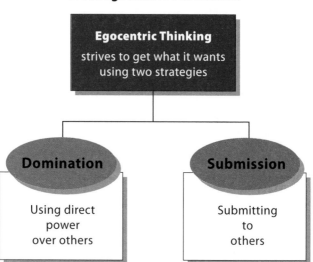

Egocentric Thinking
strives to get what it wants
using two strategies

Domination

Using direct
power
over others

Submission

Submitting
to
others

Essential Idea: **Two irrational ways to gain and use power are given in two distinct forms of egocentric strategy:**

1) The art of dominating others (a direct means to getting what one wants).

2) The art of submitting to others (an indirect means to getting what one wants).

Insofar as we are thinking egocentrically, we seek to satisfy our egocentric desires either directly or indirectly, by exercising power and control over others, or by submitting to those who can act to serve our interest. To put it crudely, egocentric behavior either bullies or grovels. It either threatens those weaker or subordinates itself to those more powerful, or oscillates between them in subtle maneuvers and schemes.

                    www.criticalthinking.org

The Logic of Egocentric Domination

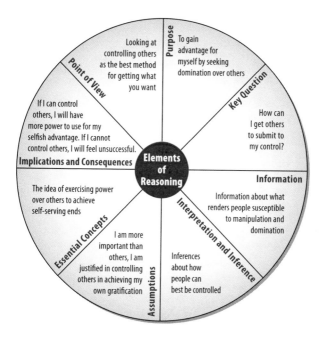

Purpose
To gain advantage for myself by seeking domination over others

Key Question
How can I get others to submit to my control?

Information
Information about what renders people susceptible to manipulation and domination

Interpretation and Inference
Inferences about how people can best be controlled

Assumptions
I am more important than others, I am justified in controlling others in achieving my own gratification

Essential Concepts
The idea of exercising power over others to achieve self-serving ends

Implications and Consequences
If I can control others, I will have more power to use for my selfish advantage. If I cannot control others, I will feel unsuccessful.

Point of View
Looking at controlling others as the best method for getting what you want

Elements of Reasoning

The Logic of Egocentric Submission

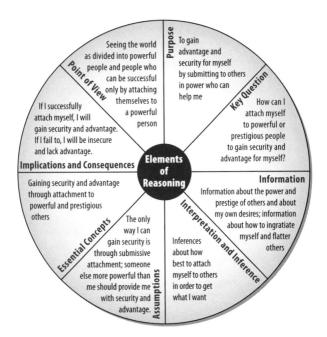

Purpose: To gain advantage and security for myself by submitting to others in power who can help me

Key Question: How can I attach myself to powerful or prestigious people to gain security and advantage for myself?

Information: Information about the power and prestige of others and about my own desires; information about how to ingratiate myself and flatter others

Interpretation and Inference: Inferences about how best to attach myself to others in order to get what I want

Assumptions: The only way I can gain security is through submissive attachment; someone else more powerful than me should provide me with security and advantage.

Essential Concepts: Gaining security and advantage through attachment to powerful and prestigious others

Implications and Consequences: If I successfully attach myself, I will gain security and advantage. If I fail, I will be insecure and lack advantage.

Point of View: Seeing the world as divided into powerful people and people who can be successful only by attaching themselves to a powerful person

Elements of Reasoning

      www.criticalthinking.org

Pathological Dispositions of the Human Mind

An array of interrelated pathological dispositions are inherent in native egocentric thought. To significantly develop as rational persons, we must identify these tendencies in our lives, determining which of them are the most prominent and which the least problematic. As you read them, ask yourself whether you recognize these as processes that occur in your own mind (if you conclude, "not me!" think again):

- **egocentric memory:** the natural tendency to "forget" evidence and information that do not support our thinking and to "remember" evidence and information that do

- **egocentric myopia:** the natural tendency to think in an absolutist way within an overly narrow point of view

- **egocentric righteousness:** the natural tendency to see ourselves in possession of "The Truth"

- **egocentric hypocrisy:** the natural tendency to ignore flagrant inconsistencies—between what we profess to believe and the actual beliefs our behavior implies, or between the standards we apply to ourselves and those we apply to others

- **egocentric oversimplification:** the natural tendency to ignore real and important complexities in the world in favor of simplistic notions when consideration of those complexities would require us to modify our beliefs or values

- **egocentric blindness:** the natural tendency to not notice facts and evidence that contradict our favored beliefs or values

- **egocentric immediacy:** the natural tendency to over-generalize immediate feelings and experiences, so that when one, or only a few, events in our life seem highly favorable or unfavorable, all of life seems favorable or unfavorable to us

- **egocentric absurdity:** the natural tendency to fail to notice when our thinking has "absurd" implications

Challenging the Pathological Dispositions of the Human Mind

It is not enough to recognize abstractly that the human mind has a predictable pathology. We must take concrete steps to correct it. This requires us to develop the habit of identifying these tendencies in action. We can all perform these corrections, but only over time and with deliberate practice.

Correcting egocentric memory. We can correct our natural tendency to "forget" evidence and information that do not support our thinking and to "remember" evidence and information that do, by overtly seeking evidence and information that do not support our thinking and directing explicit attention to them. If you try and cannot find such evidence, you should assume you have not conducted your search properly.

Correcting egocentric myopia. We can correct our natural tendency to think in an absolutistic way within an overly narrow point of view by routinely thinking within points of view that conflict with our own. For example, if we are liberal, we can take the time to read books by insightful conservatives. If we are conservative, we can take the time to read books by insightful liberals. If we are North Americans, we can study a contrasting South American point of view or a European or Far-Eastern or Middle-Eastern or African point of view. By the way, if you don't discover significant personal prejudices through this process, you should question whether you are acting in good faith in trying to identify your prejudices.

Correcting egocentric righteousness. We can correct our natural tendency to feel superior in light of our confidence that we possess the truth by regularly reminding ourselves how little we actually know. In this case, we can explicitly state the unanswered questions that surround whatever knowledge we may have. By the way, if you don't discover that there is much more that you do not know than you do, you should question the manner in which you pursued your own ignorance.

Correcting egocentric hypocrisy. We can correct our natural tendency to ignore flagrant inconsistencies between what we profess to believe and the actual beliefs our behavior implies, and inconsistencies between the standards to which we hold ourselves and those to which we hold others. We can do this by regularly comparing the criteria and standards by which we are judging others with those by which we are judging ourselves. If you don't find many flagrant inconsistencies in your own thinking and behavior, you should doubt the accuracy of your search.

Correcting egocentric oversimplification. We can correct our natural tendency to ignore real and important complexities in the world by regularly focusing on those complexities, formulating them explicitly in words, and targeting them. If you don't discover over time that you have oversimplified many important issues, you should question whether you have really confronted the complexities inherent in the issues.

Correcting egocentric blindness. We can correct our natural tendency to ignore facts or evidence that contradict our favored beliefs or values by explicitly seeking out those facts and evidence. If you don't find yourself experiencing significant discomfort as you pursue these facts, you should question whether you are taking them seriously. If you discover that your traditional beliefs were all correct from the beginning, you probably moved to a new and more sophisticated level of self-deception.

Correcting egocentric immediacy. We can correct our natural tendency to over-generalize immediate feelings and experiences by getting into the habit of putting positive and negative events into a larger perspective. You can temper the negative events by reminding yourself of how much you have that many others lack. You can temper the positive events by reminding yourself of how much is yet to be done, of how many problems remain. You know you are keeping an even keel if you find that you have the energy to act effectively in either negative or positive circumstances. You know that you are falling victim to your emotions if and when you are immobilized by them.

Correcting egocentric absurdity. We can correct our natural tendency to ignore thinking that has absurd consequences by making the consequences of our thinking explicit and assessing them for their realism. This requires that we frequently trace the implications of our beliefs and their consequences in our behavior. For example, we should frequently ask ourselves: "If I really believed this, how would I act? Do I really act that way?"

By the way, personal ethics is a fruitful area for disclosing egocentric absurdity. We frequently act in ways that are "absurd"—given what we insist we believe in. If, after what you consider to be a serious search, you find no egocentric absurdity in your life, think again. You are probably self-deceived.

Defense Mechanisms of the Mind

The human mind routinely engages in unconscious processes that are egocentrically motivated, and that strongly influence our behavior. When functioning egocentrically, we seek to get what we want. We see the world from a narrow self-serving perspective. Yet we also see ourselves as driven by purely rational motives. We therefore disguise our egocentric motives as those that appear rational. This disguise necessitates self-deception.

Self-deception is achieved by means of defense mechanisms. The concept of defense mechanisms was first developed by Sigmund and Anna Freud. Defense mechanisms overlap and interrelate with intellectual pathologies as well as with informal fallacies. Here are some of the most common defense mechanisms:

Denial: When a person refuses to believe undisputable evidence or facts in order to maintain a favorable self-image or favored set of beliefs. A basketball player, for example, may deny that there are any real flaws in his game in order to maintain an image of himself as highly skilled at basketball. A "patriot" may deny—in the face of clear-cut evidence—that his country ever violates human rights or acts unjustly.

Identification: When a person takes to himself those qualities and ideals he admires in other people and institutions. Through sociocentric identification he elevates his sense of worth. Examples: a football fan experiencing an inner sense of triumph when his team wins, a parent experiencing a triumph in the success of his children, a citizen feeling elevated by the triumph of his nation's armed forces.

Projection: When a person attributes to another person what he or she feels or thinks in order to avoid unacceptable thoughts and feelings. A wife who doesn't love her husband may accuse him of not loving her (when he really does) in order to unconsciously deal with her dishonesty in the relationship.

Repression: When thoughts, feelings or memories unacceptable to the individual are prevented from reaching consciousness. This often occurs when memories are considered too painful to remember. It can also be a form of "forgetting" because the person doesn't want to remember something unpleasant (such as a dental appointment).

Rationalization: When a person gives reasons (sometimes good reasons) for his behavior, but not the true reasons, because his actions result from unconscious motives he cannot consciously accept. The father who beats his children may rationalize his behavior by saying he is doing it for his children's "own good," so they will become more disciplined, when the true reason is that he has lost control of his behavior.

Stereotyping: When a person lumps people together based on some common characteristic, forming a rigid, biased perception of the group and the individuals in the group. One form of stereotyping comes from cultural bias wherein the person assumes that practices and beliefs in his culture are superior to those in other cultures simply by virtue of being part of his culture. He takes his group to be the measure of all groups and people.

Scapegoating: When a person attempts to avoid criticism of himself by blaming another person, group or thing for his or her own mistakes or faults.

Sublimation: When a person diverts instinctive, primitive or socially unacceptable desires into socially acceptable activities. The sexually unfulfilled drill sergeant may sublimate his sexual energy through aggressive and dominating behavior toward new recruits.

Wishful Thinking: When a person unconsciously misinterprets facts in order to maintain a belief. Wishful thinking leads to false expectations and usually involves seeing things more positively than is reasonable in the situation.

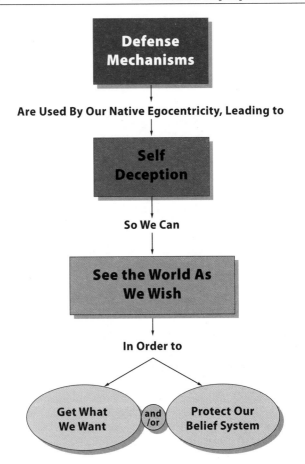

Defense Mechanisms

Are Used By Our Native Egocentricity, Leading to

Self Deception

So We Can

See the World As We Wish

In Order to

Get What We Want   and/or   Protect Our Belief System

Popular Misunderstandings of the Mind

It is common to believe (erroneously) that:

- Emotion and reason often conflict with each other.
- Emotion and reason function independently of each other.
- It is possible to be an emotional person and hence do little reasoning.
- It is possible to be a rational person and hence experience little emotion.
- Rational persons are cold and mechanical, like Mr. Spock.
- Emotional persons are lively, energetic, warm, but poor reasoners.

In These Mistaken Views:

1. One must give up the possibility of a rich emotional life if one decides to become a rational person.
2. One must give up rationality if one is to live a passionate life.

These Misunderstandings:

- Lead us to think of thought and emotion as if they were oil and water rather than inseparable functions of mind.
- Lead us away from realizing the thinking underlying our emotions and the emotions that influence our thinking.
- Lead us to think that there is nothing we can do to control our emotional life.

　　www.criticalthinking.org

Emotional Intelligence and Critical Thinking

Emotion: A state of consciousness having to do with the arousal of feelings. Refers to any of the personal reactions, pleasant or unpleasant, that one may have in a situation.

Intelligence: The ability to learn or understand from experience or to respond successfully to new experiences, the ability to acquire and retain knowledge. Implies the use of reason in solving problems and directing conduct effectively.

Emotional Intelligence: Bringing intelligence to bear upon emotions. Guiding emotions through high quality reason. Implies that high quality reasoning in a situation will lead to more satisfactory emotional states than low quality reasoning.

Critical Thinking provides the link between:

Intelligence   ⟷   Emotion

Critical Thinking:

- brings intelligence to bear upon our emotional life
- enables us to take command of our emotions
- enables us to make good judgments
- provides us with a satisfactory emotional life

Essential Idea: When our thinking is of high quality, rational emotions follow. When we develop rational emotions, we think reasonably.

Some Basic Definitions

Affect: The dimension of the mind comprised of emotions and desires. Affect is the counterpart to cognition.

Cognition: The dimension of the mind that thinks. Through cognition we make sense of the world. We figure things out. We make assumptions, inferences and judgments. We interpret situations and experiences. We conceptualize, we formulate ideas. Cognition is the counterpart to affect.

Critical Thinking: A disciplined, self-directed cognitive process leading to high quality decisions and judgments through the analysis, assessment and reformulation of thinking. It presupposes understanding of the parts of thinking, or elements of reasoning, as well as the intellectual standards by which reasoning is assessed and intellectual traits which dispose us to think in deep and honest ways.

Defense Mechanism: A self-deceptive process used by the mind to avoid dealing with unpleasant realities such as accepting responsibility for one's actions, or giving up a selfish desire while deceiving oneself into thinking one's behavior is rational and one's thinking justifiable. Through the use of defense mechanisms the mind can avoid conscious recognition of negative feelings such as guilt, pain, anxiety, etc.

Egocentrism: Any mental state derived from self-deception and leading to irrational behavior and/or emotions. It involves thinking that systematically excludes, ignores or violates the rights and needs of others or keeps one trapped in a dysfunctional self-destructive frame of mind. Egocentrism is the native condition of the undeveloped, uncultivated mind.

Egocentric Domination: The egocentric tendency of the mind to seek what it wants through the irrational use of direct power over, or intimidation of, people. Egocentric domination, or "top dog" behavior may be overt or covert. On the one hand, dominating egocentrism can involve harsh, dictatorial, tyrannical, or bullying behavior (e.g., a physically abusive spouse). On the other hand, it might involve subtle messages and behavior that imply the use of control or force if "necessary" (e.g., a supervisor reminding a subordinate, by quiet innuendo, that his or her employment is contingent upon unquestioning obedience).

Egocentric Submission: The egocentric tendency of the mind to join and serve people it deems as more powerful as a means of getting what it wants. Egocentric submission is the opposite of egocentric domination. Using this form of "underdog thinking," the person joins and serves more powerful others, who then: (1) give one a sense of personal importance, (2) protect one, and (3) share with one some of the benefits of their success. The irrational person uses both egocentric domination and submission, though not to the same extent. Those who seem to be more successful in submitting to more powerful others tend to do so. Those who seem to be more successful in using overt force and control tend to dominate. Submissive behavior can be seen publicly in the relationship of rock stars or sport stars to their admiring followers. Most social groups have an internal "pecking order," with some playing roles of leader and most playing roles of followers. A fair-minded rational person seeks neither to dominate nor to irrationally submit to others.

Egocentric Immediacy: The irrational tendency noted by Piaget wherein a person over-generalizes from a set of positive or negative events to either a "Isn't life wonderful" or "Isn't life awful" state of mind. Instead of accurately interpreting situations, the mind over-generalizes, seeing the world either in sweeping negative or positive terms.

Emotional Intelligence: Bringing intelligence to bear upon emotions. Guiding emotions through high quality reason. Implies that high quality reasoning in a situation will lead to more satisfactory emotional states than low quality reasoning.

Human Mind: The processes created by the brain comprised of cognition and affect, more particularly: thinking, feeling and wanting. These processes can be conscious or unconscious.

Irrationality: The mind's use of evidence and reasoning in the attempt either to gain unjustified advantage over others, or to maintain an unjustified self image, or to hide a dysfunctional mental state or posture.

Pathological Dispositions: Innate tendencies of the human mind created by native egocentrism and leading to systematic distortion of reality. The pathological dispositions of mind often result in unethical, harmful thoughts and behavior. These dispositions are the opposite of intellectual dispositions such as intellectual integrity, intellectual humility, intellectual perseverance, intellectual courage, intellectual autonomy, and intellectual sense of justice.

Rationality: The mind's appropriate use of evidence and reasoning in the attempt to see things objectively and act in accordance with what is reasonable in the situation.

Self-Deception: The natural human tendency to deceive oneself about one's true motivations, character, or identity. This phenomenon is so common to humans that the human species might well be defined "the self-deceiving animal." Through self-deception, humans are able to ignore unpleasant realities and problems in their thinking and behavior. Self-deception reinforces self-righteousness and intellectual arrogance. It enables us to pursue selfish interests while disguising our motives as altruistic or reasonable. Through self-deception, humans have "justified," and continue to justify, flagrantly unethical acts, policies, and practices. All humans engage in self-deception—but not to the same degree.

Sociocentrism: An extension of egocentric identity from the self ("I am superior") to the group ("We are superior"). It occurs naturally in the human mind and is based on the assumption that one's own social group is inherently and self-evidently superior to all others (since "we" belong to it). When members of a group or society see their group as superior, and so consider the group's views as self-evidently correct and their actions self-evidently justified, they have a tendency to project this superiority into all of their thinking and, thus, to think closed-mindedly and simplistically. Dissent and doubt are then considered disloyal and irresponsible. Those who question the group are made the object of suspicion or scorn. There is no society known to the authors that does not foster sociocentrism under the guise of patriotism.

The Thinker's Guide Library

The Thinker's Guide series provides convenient, inexpensive, portable references that students and faculty can use to improve the quality of studying, learning, and teaching. Their modest cost enables instructors to require them of all students (in addition to a textbook). Their compactness enables students to keep them at hand whenever they are working in or out of class. Their succinctness serves as a continual reminder of the most basic principles of critical thinking.

For Students & Faculty

 Critical Thinking—The essence of critical thinking concepts and tools distilled into a 22-page pocket-size guide. **#520m**

 Analytic Thinking—This guide focuses on the intellectual skills that enable one to analyze anything one might think about — questions, problems, disciplines, subjects, etc. It provides the common denominator between all forms of analysis. **#595m**

 Asking Essential Questions—Introduces the art of asking essential questions. It is best used in conjunction with the Miniature Guide to Critical Thinking and the Thinker's Guide on How to Study and Learn. **#580m**

 How to Study & Learn—A variety of strategies—both simple and complex—for becoming not just a better student, but also a master student. **#530m**

 How to Read a Paragraph—This guide provides theory and activities necessary for deep comprehension. Imminently practical for students. **#525m**

 How to Write a Paragraph—Focuses on the art of substantive writing. How to say something worth saying about something worth saying something about. **#535m**

 The Human Mind—Designed to give the reader insight into the basic functions of the human mind and to how knowledge of these functions (and their interrelations) can enable one to use one's intellect and emotions more effectively. **#570m**

 Foundations of Ethical Reasoning—Provides insights into the nature of ethical reasoning, why it is so often flawed, and how to avoid those flaws. It lays out the function of ethics, its main impediments, and its social counterfeits. **#585m**

 How to Detect Media Bias and Propaganda—Designed to help readers come to recognize bias in their nation's news and to recognize propaganda so that they can reasonably determine what media messages need to be supplemented, counter-balanced or thrown out entirely. It focuses on the internal logic of the news as well as societal influences on the media. **#575m**

 Scientific Thinking—The essence of scientific thinking concepts and tools. It focuses on the intellectual skills inherent in the well-cultivated scientific thinker. **#590m**

 Fallacies: The Art of Mental Trickery and Manipulation—Introduces the concept of fallacies and details 44 foul ways to win an argument. **#533m**

 Engineering Reasoning—Contains the essence of engineering reasoning concepts and tools. For faculty it provides a shared concept and vocabulary. For students it is a thinking supplement to any textbook for any engineering course. **#573m**

 Glossary of Critical Thinking Terms & Concepts—Offers a compendium of more than 170 critical thinking terms for faculty and students. **#534m**